D1511699

Petit Pierre
and the
Floating Marsh

In memory of my loving mother, Evern. - JD

For Lily, who always inspires me. - HS

Copyright © 2016
By Johnette Downing

Illustrations copyright © 2016
By Audubon Nature Institute
All rights reserved

ISBN: 9781455622795
E-book ISBN: 9781455622801

Printed in Malaysia
Published by Pelican Publishing Company, Inc.
1000 Burmaster Street, Gretna, Louisiana 70053

Petit Pierre
and the
Floating Marsh

Written by Johnette Downing

Illustrated by Heather Stanley

Pelican Publishing Company
GRETNA 2016

Way down south in *Louisiane,*
there is a floating marsh, a wetland.

The French word for Louisiana is *Louisiane.*

Gators and critters will tell you the story
about one little pelican that was in a quandary.

The floating marsh, also known as "flotant" marsh, refers to entangled roots of plant life
that float on the water and are not attached to soil.

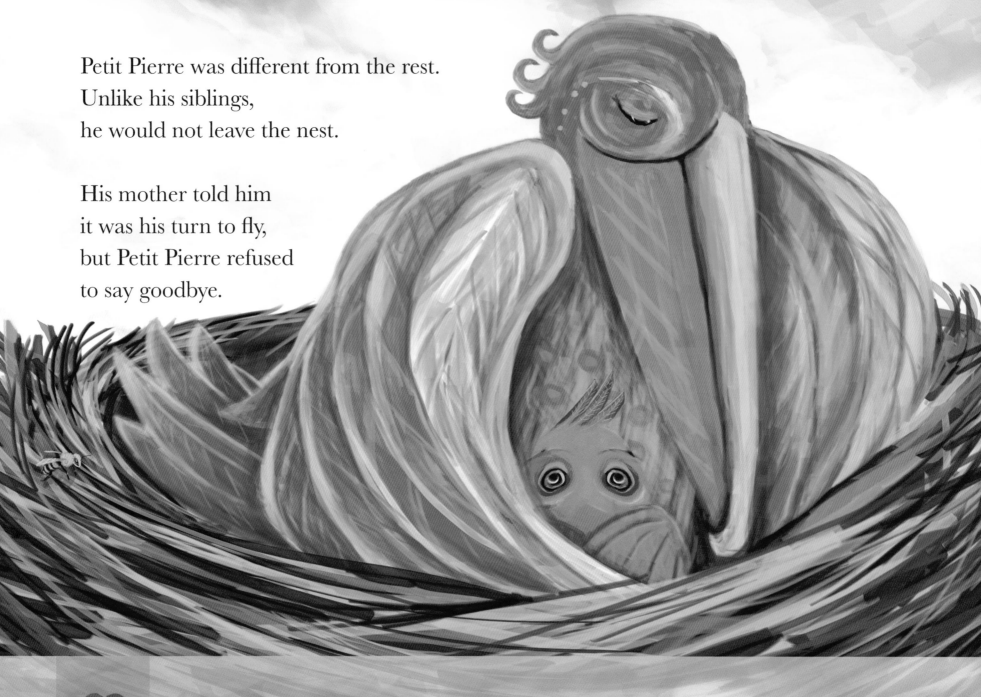

Petit Pierre was different from the rest.
Unlike his siblings,
he would not leave the nest.

His mother told him
it was his turn to fly,
but Petit Pierre refused
to say goodbye.

Wetlands are areas of land that are partially or seasonally saturated with water.

"You are all grown up," his mother said.
"You are not a chick anymore.
You need a new home.
Now go out and explore."

 These diverse ecosystems are home to animals and plants, and they serve as water filters and buffer zones to protect against storm surge, flooding, and shoreline erosion.

"But where will I live?
Where will I go,"
he asked his mother, who said,
"You will know when you know.
Just remember, wherever you roam,
friends and family are what make
a home."

 The brown pelican is the Louisiana state bird.

So with a loving nudge
she sent him on his way
across the Southern sky
into the unfolding day.

Baby pelicans are called chicks, and a group of pelicans is called a pod.

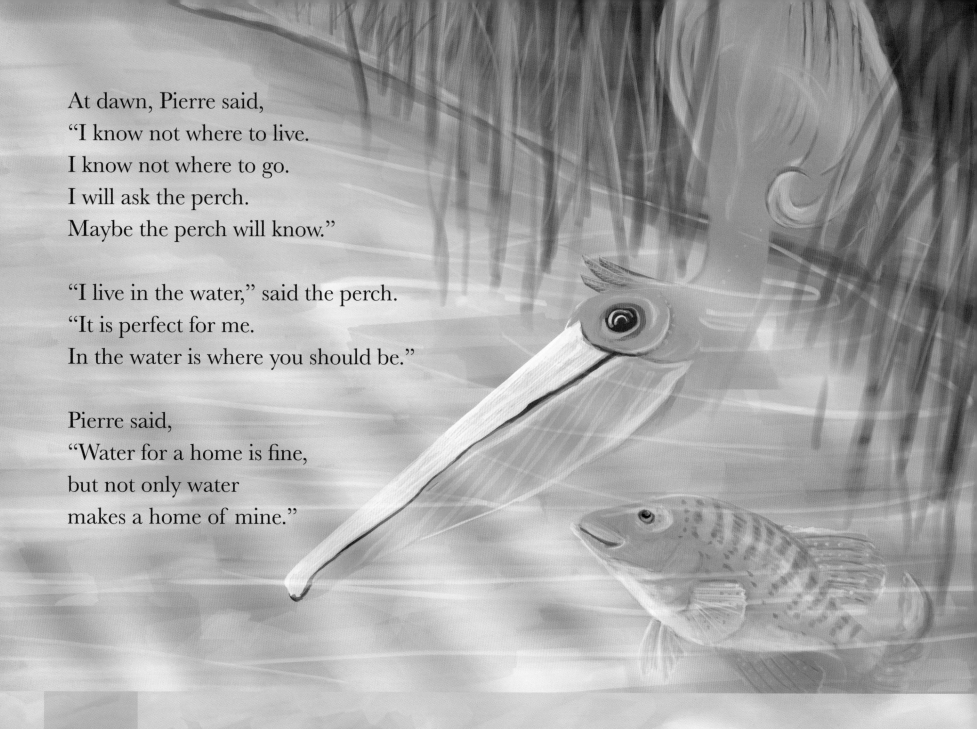

At dawn, Pierre said,
"I know not where to live.
I know not where to go.
I will ask the perch.
Maybe the perch will know."

"I live in the water," said the perch.
"It is perfect for me.
In the water is where you should be."

Pierre said,
"Water for a home is fine,
but not only water
makes a home of mine."

 The Louisiana state freshwater fish is the white perch, also known as the white crappie.

Giving Pierre a drop of water,
the perch sent him on his way
across the Southern sky
into the unfolding day.

The Cajun French term for white perch is *sac-au-lait* or "sack of milk" because of its white belly.

In the twilight, Pierre said,
"I know not where to live.
I know not where to go.
I will ask the crawfish.
Maybe the crawfish will know."

"I live in the mud," said the crawfish.
"It is perfect for me.
In the mud is where you should be."

Pierre said,
"Mud for a home is fine,
but not only mud
makes a home of mine."

The Louisiana state crustacean, the crawfish, builds its home in the mud by digging a tunnel and depositing pellets or balls of mud in a tall cylinder chimney encircling the tunnel entrance.

Giving Pierre a ball of mud,
the crawfish sent him on his way
across the Southern sky
into the unfolding day.

Burrowed inside the tunnel, the crawfish is protected from predators.

At sunrise, Pierre said,
"I know not where to live.
I know not where to go.
I will ask the egret.
Maybe the egret will know."

"I live in the reeds," said the egret.
"It is perfect for me.
In the reeds is where you should be."

Pierre said,
"Reeds for a home are fine,
but not only reeds
make a home of mine."

The slender snowy egret, with its distinctive yellow feet and snow-white plumage,
slowly wades in canals bordered by tall cane-like reeds known as Roseau or Rouseau cane.

Giving Pierre a slender reed,
the egret sent him on his way
across the Southern sky
into the unfolding day.

 Rouseau cane plays a major role in building coastal wetlands and stabilizing the marsh by breaking waves and capturing sediment.

In the early morning, Pierre said,
"I know not where to live.
I know not where to go.
I will ask the heron.
Maybe the heron will know."

"I live near the lotus," said the heron.
"It is perfect for me.
Near the lotus is where you should be."

Pierre said,
"Near the lotus for a home is fine,
but not only the lotus
makes a home of mine."

 The tricolored heron, also known as the Louisiana heron, is a water-wading bird
with a distinctive white belly and contrasting striped markings on the underside of its neck.

Giving Pierre a lotus,
the heron sent him on his way
across the Southern sky
into the unfolding day.

 The American lotus, also known as the Cajun peanut or *graine à voler*, is an edible, flowering aquatic plant.

At midmorning, Pierre said,
"I know not where to live.
I know not where to go.
I will ask the black bear.
Maybe the black bear will know."

"I live in a cypress tree,"
said the black bear.
"It is perfect for me.
In a cypress tree
is where you should be."

Pierre said,
"A cypress tree for a home is fine,
but not only a cypress tree
makes a home of mine."

 The Louisiana state mammal is the black bear.

Giving Pierre a cypress seedling,
the black bear sent him on his way
across the Southern sky
into the unfolding day.

 The black bear often makes its home in the Louisiana state tree, the water-resistant bald cypress.

At noon, Pierre said,
"I know not where to live.
I know not where to go.
I will ask the turtle.
Maybe the turtle will know."

"I live in a sunny spot," said the turtle.
"It is perfect for me. In a sunny spot
is where you should be."

Pierre said,
"A sunny spot for a home is fine,
but not only a sunny spot
makes a home of mine."

 The red-eared slider is the most abundant turtle in the Louisiana coastal wetlands.

Giving Pierre a spot of sun,
the turtle sent him on his way
across the Southern sky
into the unfolding day.

The red-eared slider can often be found on partially submerged logs drying out its shell
and warming its body in the hot Southern sun.

In the late afternoon, Pierre said,
"I know not where to live.
I know not where to go.
I will ask the muskrat.
Maybe the muskrat will know."

"I live in the grass," said the muskrat.
"It is perfect for me.
In the grass is where you should be."

Pierre said,
"Grass for a home is fine,
but not only grass
makes a home of mine."

The common muskrat prefers a wetland meal of three-cornered grass with triangular stems.

Giving Pierre a blade of grass,
the muskrat sent him on his way
across the Southern sky
into the unfolding day.

Grasses help build land in the wetland through a cycle of regeneration (growing and decaying vegetation).

At dusk, Pierre said,
"I know not where to live.
I know not where to go.
I will ask the alligator.
Maybe the alligator will know."

The wise old alligator said,
"Petit Pierre, I have watched you
fly around all day looking for
a home, but you have found none.
Open your eyes and listen to
your heart. With their gifts,
your friends and family have
given you all you need to make
a fresh start. I live in this wetland.
It is perfect for me. In this beautiful
wetland is where you too should be."

 The Louisiana state reptile, the American alligator, is the largest reptile in North America.

 The American alligator helps maintain the structure of wetland ecosystems through the building of burrows that provide homes for other animals.

For the first time, Pierre stopped
and looked at his surroundings.

He saw the perch in the water,

the crawfish in the mud,

the egret in the reeds,

the heron near the lotus,

the black bear in the cypress tree,

the turtle in the sun,

the muskrat in the grass,

the alligator,

and his family

living together in the wetland.

Petit Pierre said,
"I know exactly where to live!
I know exactly where to go!
The wetland for a home is fine.
It perfectly makes
a home of mine."

Giving Pierre a little wisdom,
the alligator sent him on his way
across the Southern sky
into the ending day
to make a home so grand
near his friends and family
in the floating marsh—the wetland.

Friend a Pelican
Be a Wetland MVP and Take the Pledge

The Louisiana wetlands are fragile ecosystems where all of the flora, fauna, and humans depend upon one another for survival, each playing a vital role in creating a harmonious, healthy, and balanced habitat or home. It takes a community to make a home, with each person doing their small part for the greater good.

Working together with your friends and family, you too can help Petit Pierre make a home in the wetland. In the story, each animal friend gives Petit Pierre a special gift to build his wetland home: water, mud, a reed, a lotus, a cypress seedling, sun, grass, and wisdom.

One Person Can Make a Difference

Beginning today, I promise to protect the wetlands
by doing two or more of the following actions:

- Practice the three *R*'s—Reduce, Reuse, and Recycle!

- Participate in programs that help protect and restore wetlands,
  like a beach clean-up or wetland planting project.

- Pick up litter to keep trash out of the wetlands.

- Plant native species such as live oak, cypress, tupelo, red maple,
  green ash, hackberry, spartina (cord grass or wiregrass),
  Rouseau cane, American lotus, and three-cornered grass
  to preserve the ecological balance of local wetlands.

- Use unbleached paper and recycled products whenever you can.
  Bleached paper contains toxic chemicals that can
  contaminate water.

- Share *Petit Pierre and the Floating Marsh* with friends and family.
  Proceeds from each book fund wetlands education
  programs in partnership with the New Orleans Pelicans
  and Audubon Nature Institute.

_____   _____

Your Name   Date

 The Louisiana state insect is the honeybee.